Pain Killer

Constance Roslinda Gary

Copyright © 2018, 2016 by Constance Roslinda Gary.

All rights reserved. No part of this publication may be reproduced, distributed, or transmitted in any form or by any means, including photocopying, recording, or other electronic or mechanical methods, without the prior written permission of the author, except in the case of brief quotations embodied in critical reviews and certain other noncommercial uses permitted by copyright law.

Except otherwise stated, all scripture is taken from the King James Version of the Holy Bible (Public Domain)

Printed in the United States of America

ISBN: Paperback: 978-1-948172-63-9
        eBook: 978-1-948172-62-2

Library of Congress Control Number: 2018943118

Stonewall Press
363 Paladium Court
Owings Mills, MD 21117
www.stonewallpress.com
1-888-334-0980

To the global youth community who live daily with tormenting fears and inner pains. JESUS is your ultimate, universal pain killer!

- "...I will pour out My Spirit on all flesh; Your sons and your daughters shall prophesy, Your old men shall dream dreams. Your young men shall see visions... I will pour out My Spirit..." (Joel 2:28-29)

- "Do not say, "I am a youth, For you shall go to all whom I send you, And whatsoever I command you shall speak. Do not be afraid of their faces, For I AM with you to deliver you," Say the LORD. (Jeremiah 1:7-8)

- *"Assuredly, I say to you, unless you are converted and become as little Children you will by no means enter the kingdom of heaven. "Therefore whoever humbles himself as a little child is the greatest in. The kingdom of heaven." "Whosoever receives one little child like this in MY name receives ME." (Matthew 18:3-6)*

- But JESUS said, *"Let the little children come to Me. and do not forbid them: For of such is the kingdom of heaven." (Matthew 19:14)*

VISION   12/27/85   8:00AM

White hair, deep pool blue eyes. Big tears rolling down CHRIST's face. Priorities are so wrong. Time is short. Heart is grieved. So many people Have put their priorities in wrong order. Souls are in the balance. Millions and billions are being put into mortar and brick hospital buildings. Not interested in saving souls. Not interested in temple built without hands. Souls are being lost! JESUS weeps over North America.

"Heaven and earth shall pass away…." (Matt.5:18)

As sand in the dunes of the dessert… Seven million Souls Crusade!

CONTENTS

VISION 12/27/85 8:00AM v
PREFACE xi

ALL IS WELL 1
ARE YOU ALL OPIOID UP! 4
BLESSED YOUR HOLY NAME 5
BUT JESUS SAID 7
CRACKED UP 9
CREATED 11
DANCE to the MOMENT 13
DELIVERED FROM ALL EVIL 14
DR. HEROINE 16
EMOTIONAL PAIN 17
ETERNAL SECURITY 18
FOOL HAS SAID 19
FREE BASE 20
FREE US 22
FROM NOW ON 24
GENERATION OF VIPERS 25
GLORY TO GOD! 27
GOD WILL! 28
GOD! SET US FREE! 29
HALLELUJAH! 31
HELP ME THROUGH THIS DAY 32
HIS MERCIES ENDURETH FOREVER 34

HOLY JESUS! HOLY LORD!	36
INHERITANCE OF THE RIGHTEOUS	37
I AM THAT I AM	38
I AM the GOD THAT HEALS	39
IF	41
IN SPIRIT and IN TRUTH	42
IT'S REAL	43
JESUS CAME TODAY!	44
JESUS! SOON COMING KING!	45
JESUS the Pain Killer	46
JUST SAY NO	47
KILLING FIELDS	48
LET OTHERS	50
LET THE HEALING FLOW	52
LIVING and FORGIVING	54
LORD BE MERCIFUL	55
MAN WHO	57
MISSION FOR CHRIST'S SAKE	59
MY GOD! MY GOD!	60
NEW WAVE OF MY HEALING	62
NO OTHER HELP	63
KINGDOM OF GOD	65
SURRENDERED LIFE	66
OBEDIENCE TO GOD	68
ON CALVARY	70
ONLY YOU	72
OUTCRY FROM SILENT LIPS	74
PLACE CALLED THERE	75
PRAISE!	77
PRAY!	79
REPENTANCE! RECONCILIATION!	80
SAVED BUT NOT SERIOUS	82
SOAKING IN JESUS' LOVE	84
SPIRITUAL HOMELESSNESS	85

STAND ON THE WORD 86
SUDDENLY JESUS 88
THANK GOD 90
THY WILL 92
TOUCH NOT MY ANOINTED 93
WE ARE THE CHURCH 94
WHAT IS MAN? 96
WHAT WOULD YOU HAVE ME TO DO? 98
WHERE DO WE GO FROM HERE? 100
WORSHIP HIM! 102
YOU CAN'T TAKE PLACE OF GOD 103

PREFACE

Special thanks to GOD, JESUS CHRIST, and the HOLY GHOST!
GOD's love exploded in my life!
I was engulfed in the presence of the HOLY GHOST!
It manifested through the gift of many tongues!
Poems and songs were downloaded from heaven past my mind!
Praises filled my garden of prayer!
It is with gratitude that I humbly share these poems with you!

ALL IS WELL

"I AM the resurrection, and the life: he that believeth in Me, though he were dead, yet shall he live:" (John 11:25)

All is well! She said
As she rushed to find the prophet
All is well! All is well!
She rode hurriedly searching

All is well!
"I AM the resurrection …"
All is well!
I AM the Life! (John 11:25)

The prophet rushed to her house
Prophet entered the bedroom
Stretched his body over lifeless boy
Breathe into him the breath of life

Mary and Martha don't weep
Lazarus is not dead
He is only asleep
He lay three days in the tomb

Searching for the man of GOD
As her son lay dead
All is well!
Her young son lay dead!

He that believeth on me
Though he is dead
Yet shall he live. Yes!
"I AM the resurrection…" (John 11:25)

Though he is dead
Yet shall he live
Hurry JESUS! Lazarus is dying!
Never mind he is dead.

"JESUS wept" (John 11: 35)
As Lazarus slept
Mary and Martha said,
What's the use?

Pain Killer | 1

Though he is dead
In trespasses & sin
Blinded by prince of this world
An appointed time he shall be loosed

Saul of Taurus on Damascus Road
Dead in trespass & sin
Struck blind by CHRIST' light
He shall live again.

Blinded by hatred & murder
Doubt fear & death
Religious demons
Social wealth

JESUS! The light of the world
Stopped Saul as his tracks
Knocked him off his horse
Blinded Saul sent to Cornelius' house

Saul! Saul! Why do you
Kick against the prick?
Saul! Saul! Why do you
Kick against the prick?
If you would believe
You should see the glory of GOD
Believe on the LORD JESUS
And you shall be saved!

JESUS! Son of David!
Have mercy on me!
JESUS! Son of David!
Set me free!
Blinded naturally
Blinded spiritually
Blinded in sin
Blinded in trespass

All is well! She said.
Though my son is dead
In trespass & sin
He shall live again!

Oh! Mothers! Don't you weep!
Oh! Mother! Don't you mourn!
He is only asleep! Awake! My son!
Your light has come!

CHRIST JEUSUS has come to save you!
CHRIST JESUS! His banner unfurled!
CHRIST JESUS has come to save you!
CHRIST JESUS! Faithful and true!

"For this purpose was the
Son of man manifested
To destroy the
Works of the devil…"

Deceitful lies
Destruction of self
Dishonor of parents
Disrespect of others

Bounded by youthful lust
Fort fornication & adultery
Prisoners of alcoholism
Shackles of crack, cocaine, heroine

Yes! You though dead in trespass & sin
Yes! You're blinded by the prince of this world!
Yes! You though sin abounds
Yes! You're in life's pig sty found

Satan! I rebuke you!
Devil is a liar!
Life and death
Power in your tongue

Destroy the works of Satan
Confess the LORD JESUS CHRIST!
Defeat the prince of the air
CHRIST JESUS! Come in here!

Come into my heart!
Come into my body!
Come into my temple!
Come into my home!

My boat of life is rocking
My ship is in a stormy sea!
JESUS of Nazareth said

"Peace be still!" (Mark 4:39)

Run on my son!
Run on my daughter!
*"Fight the good fight of faith...
(1 Tim. 6:12)*
CHRIST JESUS is in this place!

ARE YOU ALL OPIOID UP!

Are you all opioids up? Opioids are deadly dangerous! Let me say, it is dangerous and deadly. Dangerous, because it is definitely injurious to your health. It is deadly, because it kills ambition, determination, imagination and inspiration.

- You are young enough to dream dreams. So be ambitious enough to attain them. You are bright enough to achieve that goal that you have conceived. Even if you have already physically conceived a child, you, young mothers and fathers.
- Life is not a dead end street with dope as a "STOP" sign!
- It is up to you to say "NO!" It is up to you to act that "NO!" out.
- It is up to you whether or not you will go ahead with your life or "Go along" with the crowd
- Crowd around positive, productive people with good things and goals
- Crowd your mind with grand ideas
- Fill your mind with good words, GOD' word!

Live each day as if it is your last! Look up! Live! Be whole today!
Touching, helping others along the way! *"But seek ye first the kingdom of GOD...*
Do not off your course, purpose, stray! *All these things shall be added!"*
  (Matt.6:33)
From dope and perversion stay away! Hallelujah! Amen!

BLESSED YOUR HOLY NAME

Bless your Holy name GOD!
For all You've done in past,
 present, future
You know our needs before we ask
Our pains before we can even
 fell them

Thank You for making us in Your image
Thank You for Your bountiful treasures

Thank You for grace without measure
Thank You for our earthly pleasure

Thank You for our heavenly home

Thank You for Your only Son
Thank You for Your beloved One!
You for earth, wind & fire

Thank GOD for every breath we breathe!
Thank GOD for every twig, every seed!
Thank GOD for You, who supersedes!
Thank GOD for Your Son, who intercedes!

You, oh GOD, made all things great
 & small
You created oceans, river & water falls
You kept us least we fall
You cause thunder storms to rumble

Send flashes of lightening across skies
Just with the twinkling of Your eyes
GOD! How wondrous are You works
How wonderful are secrets of each birth

LORD! You are all & all!
GOD! Both great and small
Will confess on bended knee!
GOD! Our trust is put in Thee!

Praise GOD from whom all blessings flow
Thy will be done here below
Praise GOD! 3x Praise the LORD!
Thank GOD for His living Word!

May we, oh GOD, be a living testimony!
May we, oh GOD, seek Your face!
GOD protect us from religious phonies!
oh LORD! Send us more, more grace!

Oh GOD! My LORD! Oh, JESUS! My KING!
Oh GOD! Your Word! Oh JESUS do angels sing!
Praise the LORD! Praise GOD!
Down the road of righteousness trod!

Praise His Holy Name! 3x

Praise the LORD! Praise GOD! 3x Amen!

BUT JESUS SAID

Go away! Get out! You failed the test!
JESUS said, *"Come unto me! I'll give you rest!"* (Matt. 11:28)
You are a sinner, woman, man, boy, girl
JESUS said, "Abide in Me! Abide in My word!" *(John 15:4)*

Left out of the mainstream of life
JESUS said, *"I AM the way! Truth! Light!"* (John 14:6)
Christian zombie controlled by Satan's lies
JESUS said, *"My sheep know My voice!"* *(John 10:27)*

You with your heart so broken
But JESUS said, *"Ask! Seek! Knock!"*
You old age, gray & worn!
You must a reborn!

You foolish fools! "Choose!"
JESUS said, "Who will you serve?"
You callous, cold hearted men
JESUS said, "I shall come again!"

Wealthy, rich as can be
JESUS said, "Forsake all! Follow me!"
Diseased or bed ridden!
JESUS said, *"Take up your bed!'*

Disturbed, distraught, vexed, tormented
JESUS said, "Loose! Come out you demon!"
Insane! In bondage! In slavery
JESUS bled and died on Calvary!

And with His stripes we are healed!
With His precious blood we are covered!
With His word mysteries are revealed!
And JESUS is our soul's lover!

In JESUS you will soon discover!
In JESUS from diseases you will recover!
In JESUS is their freedom & sacrifice!
In JESUS you do not have to die twice!

In JESUS is remission of sin!	In JESUS there is no limit!
In JESUS we can begin again!	In JESUS there are no gimmicks!
In JESUS we can see the light!	In JESUS there is no jingle jangle!
In JESUS we can become CHRIST like!	In JESUS there is the only single!

A single purpose! One goal!	Conversion to CHRIST!
To have GOD's Word retold!	Inversion with Holy Ghost!
To have complete immersion!	Intrusion of GOD!
To surrender, complete conversion!	Involution of three in one!

Oh! GOD! Thank You!   Amen!

CRACKED UP

Are you cracked up?
Why don't you crack off?
What's that?
Get off Crack!

Get crack off?
How do you do that?
It's a simple, plain fact
Crack kills!

Crack Up! Crack off!
Get off Crack!
Stay away from it!
Cool! Chill! You know!

Still cool! Mellow!
Still high thrill! Tired of
Hearing friends scream!
Seeing buddies killed!

Crack off!
Crack up!
Crack down on crack!
Keep it off your back!

There is another way!
Start the search today!
Seek finer things of life
Chose life not death

Crack off! Crack out!
Barrier to productive life!
Crack down on Crack
Just say No! No! No!

No way, man!
I'd rather not!
No! Thank you!
Just Crack off!

Get out of my way
Your evil forces of life!
Get out of my sight!
You perverted demon!

Don't crack me up with that junk!
You cannot be serious!
Get out of my way!
You're making me furious!

Go! Find another flunky!
Another fool for the grave!
Go! Find another victim!
My loyalty you cannot have!

Get out of my way! You robber of my youth!
Get out of my way! I am seeking truth!
Get out of my way! You cheap fix!
Get out of my way! You're full of tricks!

Stay out of dope dungeons
Stay away from demon shadows
Stay off crack
Just say, "Crack off!"

Stay out of my way!
Evil forces from pits of hell!
Get out of my life!
You might as well!

Go away you devils & demons!
Go back to the pits of hell!
Read my lips! "CRACK OFF!"
C_R_A_C_K! It's the way it's spelled!

Get out of my way!
Evil forces of obscenity!
Get out of my way!
From here to eternity!
Amen! Amen!

CREATED

Created the universe & world His love on us did unfurl! Sent down His love from above! Created us for him to love	GOD gave only His beloved Son! Sacrificed His only begotten One! Shed His Son's precious blood on Calvary Who died, Arose to save you & me!
Mold & make us with potters' hands! Break! Shape hearts of men! Guide us with His everlasting eyes! Sends blessings from heaven on high!	GOD is not like man that He should lie Neither does He repent or give alibis! *"Your Father…gives good things!"* (Matt.7:11) *"Same yesterday and today and forever"* (Heb.13:8)

Alpha and Omega	Shield! Protect! Direct!	Sent down the living bread of life!
Everlasting Father	Strong tower! Hiding place!	Holy One! Supreme sacrifice!
Nurturing Mother	Where sin abound!	Died! Rose up from the grave! He's first!
Like none other	He sheds His grace!	Believe on Him! Neither hunger or thirst!

GOD sent His only Son to do GOD's will
Not mine, said JESUS, but Thine still
The Holy One did not suffer decay
Receive JESUS into your heart today (Jn.6:50)

Be born again!
Forgiveness of sin!
Heaven bound for eternity!
Confess JESUS! Be set free!

Free from bondages, oppression and sin!
Free to live CHRIST-like . Amen
Free from shackles and strife!
Free to have eternal life!

Free from scourge and plague!
Free to seek His face
Free from death, hell and the grave!
Free to live in GOD's grace

Thank You GOD for the gift of Your Son!
Thank You GOD for sanctified Holy One!
Thank You GOD for justification!
Thank You GOD for eternal salvation!   Amen!

Dance to the moment
This is how
Love each second you are together
Leave one another? No! Never!
Love as though your life depends on it!
Love! Love! Love! Don't forget!
Leave never!   Cleave forever!
Leave never!   Cleave forever!

DELIVERED FROM ALL EVIL

"For GOD so loved the world that HE gave…" (John 3:16)

Delivered from all evil
Saved from Satan's grip
Demons! Devils!
Sanctified! Saved! Freed! Set aside!

Snatched back from pits of hell
Shown into heavenly places to dwell
Become sons & daughters of Kings
Praise GOD! Heavenly host sing!

Learn! Listen! Look! Seek!
Don't be deceived! In hell Satan will burn!

Hallelujah! 3x Praise GOD!
JESUS! JESUS! JESUS' precious shed blood

Redemption plan manifested!
Redeeming Savior to us brought justice
GOD's mercy endures forever!
Put GOD in charge of your endeavors!

Make JESUS head of your life

HE made the supreme sacrifice
JESUS died! JESUS arose in order
That we may be saved

"…For His mercy endure forever"
(1 Chr. 16:34)
Here throughout all eternity nearer
"But seek ye first the kingdom of GOD And his righteousness…" (Matt. 6:33)

For His mercies endures forever (Ps.136:1)   Praise the LORD!
Here throughout all eternity   **GOD is LORD!**
"But seek ye first the kingdom of GOD…(Matt.6:33)   Sent JESUS from above

With your mouth confess the LORD JESUS   **GOD is love!**

JESUS will be with us until the end!   Praise the LORD!
JESUS, sweet JESUS, my dear friend!   GOD is LORD!
JESUS! JESUS! Lover of my soul!   Praise the LORD!
GOD's kingdom! Where you never grown old!   GOD is love!

"JESUS CHRIST the same yesterday, and today, and forever." **(Heb. 13:8)**
Be healed! Be set free in JESUS' name!
Be saved! Be delivered in JESUS' name!
Praise GOD! Thank You LORD! Amen! Amen! Amen! Amen! Amen! Amen! Amen!

Hallelujah! Soon coming KING!
Glory to GOD heavenly host sing!
Hallelujah!! Hallelujah! Hallelujah! Praise GOD!
Into His kingdom be accepted with a nod! Amen!

DR. HEROINE

Hey! What's up?
What's up, man?
You look bad man!
Bad stuff! Bad stuff!

Did you here about_____?
Yeah! He gone too!
What's up man?
What we gonna do? We hooked too!

Guess we gonna one day die, too!
What's up , man!
What can we do?
Hey! Listen! I got something to tell you!

How can we "Just say no!"
Hey! You! Off to jail you go?
A Million in the penitentiaries?
Where are the drug treatment centers?

      _____Amen! Amen! Hallelujah!_____

EMOTIONAL PAIN

Emotional pain
Call on JESUS! He will see you through!
Emotional trauma!! So unbearable!
Call on JESUS! He cures the incurable!

Hallelujah! Praise GOD! Hallelujah! Praise the LORD!
Hallelujah! Praise GOD! Hallelujah! Glory to His word!
Praise my LORD! Angels sing!
Glory to GOD for infallible, unshakeable Word!

With His stripes we are healed!
With His redemption, we are sealed!
With His blood, we are cleansed!
With His name, we are born again!

With His nailed-scared hands, we are set free!
With His pierced feet, we can become what GOD designed us to be!
With His love, we are purchased with a price!
With His shed blood, He became the supreme sacrifice!

Hallelujah! Hallelujah! Hallelujah! Amen!
Hallelujah! Hallelujah! Hallelujah! Set free! Born again!
Hallelujah! Hallelujah! Hallelujah! Amen!   Praise GOD!
Hallelujah! Hallelujah! Hallelujah! Forgiven of all sin!   Praise GOD! Amen

ETERNAL SECURITY

Eternal Security!
Eternal security!
Eternal security!
He's all mine! All mine!

JESUS bought it
On the cross!
JESUS paid the price!
With His life!

Mine! Mine! Mine!   Mine! Mine Mine!
It's mine! It's mine!   It's mine!

FOOL HAS SAID

"A fool has said in his heart There is no GOD!"
If so where is your money?
Where is the land of milk & honey?

Where do you go when you're lonely?
Where do you go when you're the only
Person sitting in an empty room
When you can't buy a mop or broom

When you feel your hands are so estrange
When you fold your hands & say
When you feel so disgusted
When Satan tries to eliminate you!

When you rise to another
When you fold your hands & say
My GOD, why have you left me?
While you long to be set free

Loose this bond of disenfranchisement	Glory to GOD!
Shackles od loneliness	Hallelujah!
Despair! Disgrace! Disgust!	Praise the LORD!
Disease! Disenchantment!	Praise GOD! Amen!

"Stand... loins girt about with the truth... breast plate of righteousness. And your feet shod with the preparation of peace... shield of faith, wherewith ye shall be able to quench all the fiery darts of the wicked... helmet of salvation...." (Eph. 6:14-17)

Be free with JESUS
With JESUS as your base

Free base! Free in JESUS!

Surrounded by GOD' grace

Free base with JESUS! GOD's Holy One
Free in JESUS! Base Your life on His Word!

Free base! Freed by JESUS! Glory to GOD!

Based on His precious shed blood!

Some free base with chemicals
Free base with GOD's only Son
Some free base on crack cocaine
Free base with My LORD JESUS CHRIST!

Get high in Holy Ghost power
Obtain the ultimate deliverance hour!
Get a hold of the great connection
JESUS will bring you to total subjection

Free base! Free! Free!
Free! Free base! Uh! Uh! 2x
Free in JESUS! Based on
Life of Word of GOD!

Free Base with JESUS!
Get a brand new start!
Free base! 3x
Glory! 7x Hallelujah!

Free base with JESUS!
Holy Ghost power thro you!
Stand up for CHRIST!
Keep Satan out of your life!

Free at last! GOD's wink & nod!
Free at last! Hallelujah!
Whom the gods would destroy!
First they make mad!

Get mad at the devil!
Give your heart to CHRIST!
Get mad at satan!
Turn away from evil!

Get mad at the devil!
Refused to be destroyed!
Get made at satan!
Daily read GOD's Word!

Get mad at devil! Hallelujah!
Turn away! Turn around!
Shun all works of devil!
Let Holy Ghost be your guide!

Turn away! Turn around!
Turn to CHRIST!
Soon coming KING!
Turn around! Turn again!

Be free from satan's wiles!
Hallelujah! Glory to GOD!
Snatched from pits of hell!
Give your heart to JESUS!

Stand on the Word!   JESUS on your side! Be set free! Hallelujah!   Amen

Free us, the homeless
Hostages of the streets
Homebound with nowhere to go
Help us LORD! Please?

GOD have mercy on us!
Starvation is deadly!
Homelessness is degradation
Help us, LORD! Please?

Young, old, rich, poor alike
Without shelter are all equal
We all have equal rights to
Life, liberty, pursuit of happiness

Perchance are there any vacancies?
Empty buildings in the community
Renovate! Sweet equity SRO
Set us free from street survival

Restore us to full citizens in human race
Have permanent resident clean, secure place
Submit your help and caring residence
From local government officials, if you please?

Please consider your present state
Remember! Statute of Liberty
Countless wars! Millions of lost lives!
Lost dreams! Tons of lies & alibis!

Remember our founding fathers
Remember you family, friends, lovers
But for the grace of God, there go I!
But for the grace of God, there go I!

From now on
He is with you until the end
He is here! Now!
JESUS is my eternal friend!

I have life!
I have peace!
I will not perish!
I have everlasting life!

I lay aside all malice! All guile! All envies!
All hypocrisies! All evil speaking!
Yield yourself to the LORD
Let Him live through you! Amen!

GENERATION OF VIPERS

Oh! Ye generation of vipers
Deceitfully perverted men!
Turning from lovers of GOD
To lovers of yourselves!

Where is your heart?
Who is your GOD?
What are your thoughts?
What price were you bought?

False prophets spring forth!
False messiahs spout trivias!
False gods worshiped daily!
False beliefs & doctrines!

Against women, children, lovers

What caused trivia to begin
Before babies begin to live?

Snuffed out before candles are built!

Foolish pleasure seekers
Wicked last generation!
Stressed! Burned out!
Diseased! Undisciplined!

Were you bought by devil's pay?
Have your hearts turned to stone?
Stone each other on technicalities
Chasing after rainbows & vanities!

What has turned you away
From the love of GOD?
What has caused even very
Elect to turn cold hearted?

"Let your light so shine before men...
(Matt. 5:16)
Your FATHER GOD who is in heaven
"Hallow be His name! His kingdom
come on..."
Earth in your life as it is in heaven

Let His *"will be done*
In you *"on earth*
As it is in heaven" (Matt: 6:10)
Be born again! New Birth!

Give us, LORD, Your bread
Living bread of heaven
Living. Loving Word! JESUS!
This day! Each & every day!

"Lead us not into temptations (Matt 6:13)
"But will with temptation also
Make a way to escape" (1 Cor.10:13)
FATHER! Not my will, but THINE!

"But deliver me from evil
Thine is the kingdom!
Thine is the power
Thine is the glory, forever. Amen."
(Matt 6:13)

Forever and ever! Amen!
For all power, glory and honor
Thou, GOD, art worthy
Worthy to be praised! 2x

For worthy is the lamb! 2x
Yes! JESUS is His name! 2x
Yes! Worthy is the lamb! 2x
KING JESUS is His name! 2x

Hallelujah!
Glory!
Glory to GOD!
Amen

Glory to GOD!
Our most high GOD!
Hallelujah! Praise GOD!
Precious Savior! Holy JESUS!

*"Amen! Even so, come
LORD JESUS!* (Rev. 22:20)
Praise GOD!
Hallelujah! Amen! Amen!

Praise GOD from whom
All blessings flow!
Praise GOD! Glory to GOD!
Praise the LORD! Hallelujah!
Thank You! JESUS!

Thank You! My personal Savior!
Thank You! JESUS!
Thank You! LORD!

I love You! JESUS!   Hallelujah!
We love You! LORD!   Hallelujah!
I love You! Savior!   Amen!
Praise GOD! Glory to GOD!   Amen!

GOD will defend!
GOD will guide!
GOD will protect!
GOD will supply!

Holy Ghost will comfort!
Holy Ghost will give utterance!
Holy Ghost will teach!
Holy Ghost will triumph!

JESUS will claim!
JESUS will deliver!
JESUS will redeem!
JESUS will save!

Jesus is LORD of your life!
JESUS! CHRIST! CHRIST!
JESUS paid the price!
JESUS made the sacrifice!

Oh LORD!
Oh! JESUS!
Thank You1 3x
Thank You LORD!   AMEN!

GOD set us free! 3x Glory to GOD!
GOD have mercy on me! Hallelujah! 3x
With the gospel of preparation of
Peace our feet are shod

In righteousness, truth & justice You do right!
JESUS CHRIST! Our Savior! Soon coming KING!
With mercy & everlasting life
Your only begotten Son sent from above!

With the love of GOD we linger here below
We take the name of JESUS everywhere we go
We send our prayer messages daily!
We drink living water freely!

Hallelujah! Praise GOD!
Hallelujah! Glory to GOD!
JESUS' precious blood
Gospel of peace our feet shod

Hallelujah! Praise GOD!
Fill us with Your infallible Word
Heal us with outstretched hands
Heal us GOD! Heal our land!

Amen & Amen!   **Hallelujah! Praise GOD!**   **Amen!**

Hallelujah! JESUS!
Praise Your Holy name
Wonderful sweet JESUS!
Yesterday, today, forever…

Glory to GOD in the highest!
Praise Your Holy name!
Glory to GOD in the highest!
Yesterday, today, forever the same

Hallelujah! Praise the LORD!
JESUS! Anointed KING! Living Word!
JESUS! Word made flesh!
JESUS! Help me do my best!

Hallelujah! Glory to GO!
Christians… feet shod…
And glow with GOD's
Holy Ghost holiness

Hallelujah! Glory to GOD!
_Praise! Sing! Read the Word!
Hallelujah! Praise the LORD
"with gospel your feet are shod…"

Bible! Love letters from GOD!
JESUS! GOD's living Word!
GOD's only begotten Son
JESUS! GOD's anointed One

Hallelujah! Praise GOD!
Hallelujah! Praise the LORD!
Hallelujah! Praise GOD

Amen! Praise GOD!
Amen! Hallelujah!
Amen! Praise GOD!

Help me thro' this day
Help me see the Creator's way
Let me know you really care
Let me feel you're really there

Walk with me! LORD!
Hold me! LORD!
Be my ever present guide!
Least me footsteps side!

Hallelujah! 4x Praise the LORD!
KING JESUS! 2x Our everlasting LORD!
From here to eternity!
O! GOD Keep Your eye on me!

Hallelujah! 3x Glory to Thee!
All power, honor, LORD let me see!
Let me feel Your tender touch
We need more of Your love so much!

Hold me fast to your bosom, please!
Do not ever leave or forsake me
Do not ever cast me aside
After all I am CHRIST JESUS' bride

Keep me JESUS ever by Your side
Holy Ghost continue be my guide
Hallelujah! 4x Praise His name
Yesterday, today, forever the same

Your eye passes over me
JESUS was sent to die for us
HE redeemed us upon Calvary's tree
His shed precious blood set us free

Hallelujah! Praises to Your name
Praise GOD heavenly host sing
Hallelujah! Heavenly host sing
KING JESUS, hallelujah, is His name

Gospel of peace of preparation Your feet must be shod Prepare! Soon coming KING!	Honor, glory, praises to Your name! Yesterday, today, forever the same! Hallelujah! 3x Praise His wonderful name!
Hallelujah! Praise GOD angels sing!	Yesterday, today, forever the same! 2x

Thanks be to GOD! Glory to our KING! Hallelujah! Heavenly host sing! Praise the LORD! We daily sing! Hallelujah! Praise GOD angels sing!	LORD! GOD! Why have Your forsaken! Devils & his demons are shaking me Living Word! JESUS CHRIST! Only You! Oh! GOD are so divine!

Help me LORD GOD JEHOVAH to walk in Your will,
not mine! Hallelujah! 3x Praise GOD!

"…upon this rock I will build My church and the gates
of hell shall not prevail…" (Matt.16:18)

HIS MERCIES ENDURETH FOREVER

"Put on the whole armor of GOD..." (Eph. 6:11)
"And your feet shod with the preparation of the gospel of peace ..." (Eph. 6:15)

When in a strange land
He leads us with an outstretched hand
When laying on a sick bed
Sickness, infirmity, diseases before Him fled
When hungry with nothing to eat
GOD' banquet table we have a seat
When pursued by enemies & friends
JESUS is with us until the end

When naked, shelter less
Without shoes on your feet
JESUS! You with a smile
Me JESUS will greet!

When rejected & criticized by man
JESUS is always your one true friend!
When abused, used & persecuted
JESUS is in His army! HE can use!

Glory! Glory! Glory! Hallelujah! Praise GOD
GOD sent His Son, JESUS, the living Word!
KING of Kings! Hallelujah! Praise GOD!
JESUS' precious shed blood! *3x Amen!*

For the remission of sins!
Receive His forgiveness! Be born again!
Hallelujah! 3x   Praise the LORD!
Read daily the bible, GOD's word!

Holy sanctified!	Hallelujah! 3x Praise the LORD
Three in One	Hallelujah! 3x Praise GOD!
Bless GOD!	Hallelujah! 3x Praise the LORD!
Shower us with blessing from above!	Hallelujah! 3x Praise GOD

Holy JESUS! Holy LORD!
Holy Spirit! Draw near!
Holy Spirit! Me hear!
Praise GOD!

Sweet! Sweet! Sweet!
Mysteries of life!
Holy! Holy! Holy!
Let me be JESUS' wife!

Holy Ghost! Ever constant friend!
Holy JESUS! The beginning! The end!
Holy LORD! Always! Forever! My LORD!
Great JEHOVAH! My GOD! My LORD!
Amen! Amen!

INHERITANCE OF THE RIGHTEOUS

"The inheritance of the righteous…" (Is 54:17)

I will bless those who bless you

LORD GOD! What means this?
My GOD! What is this you allow?
Hallelujah! Praise GOD!
Glory! 3x My Savior! My LORD!

JEUS! The anointed King! Come!
Sing! Praise Him now, angels sing!
Hallelujah! Praise GOD!
Gospel of peace your feet are shod!

Let you feet be shod
Holy! Holy! Holy! Art Thou LORD GOD!Glory!
Hallelujah! Praise the LORD
Glory! Hallelujah! Praise GOD!

Thank You! LORD! Thank You! JESUS!
Hallelujah! 3x Praise the LORD!
Hallelujah! 3x   Praise GOD!
In the name of JESUS!   Amen!

I AM THAT I AM

I AM that I AM! You are mine!
I AM that I AM! Your Will not mine!
I AM that I AM! Holy Almighty GOD!
I AM that I AM! "gospel of peace your feet…" (Eph. 6:15)

I AM that I AM! Praise His Holy name!
I AM that I AM! *"Yesterday, today, forever…"*
I Am that I AM! Holy omnipotent
I AM that I AM! Holy bible content!!

I AM that I AM! Praise the LORD!
I AM that I AM! Word made flesh!
I AM that I AM! JESUS made flesh!
I AM that I AM! JESUS is LORD!

I AM that I AM! Hallelujah! LORD of Lords!
I AM that I AM! Praise Your Holy Word!
I AM that I AM! Herds of people to Your throne
I AM that I AM! From pastures. No more to roam!

Praise GOD! Glory to GOD!
Hallelujah! JESUS is LORD!
Praise You JESUS! My GOD!
Praise You JESUS! Praise the LORD! 7x
Praise You JESUS!   Praise GOD!   Amen!

I AM the GOD THAT HEALS

I AM the LORD GOD
That heals you
I AM that I AM
Is calling me!

All our iniquities
All our sins forgiven
Our spiritual infirmities
Our illnesses, GOD heals

All our passions & secret sins
All our desires. We belong to Him
All our wants & needs
All of our yearnings!

Turn your lives over to CHRIST
Turn to JESUS! Supreme sacrifice!
Turn to JESUS! Author and Finisher
Turn to JESUS! Take rightful place!

At His feet! Clothed in your right mind!
At His throne! Seeking His will not mine!
At His grave site! Looking into empty tomb!
At His resurrection! Where there' no gloom!

No gloom!" *O death where is your sting?*
O grave, where is your victory? (1 Cor.15:55)
JESUS CHRIST! Paid it all! It's true!
For us to collect our fringe benefits!

Start today! Work for JESUS!
Start up! Paid the same wage!
He saved me! "...*nevertheless,*
Not as I will, but as Thou wilt."
(Matt. 26:39)

Amen!

If you love Me---obey me

If you're a child of GOD- walk in the fullness of My principals
If I AM your Father, my Abba- you must become fully saturated in the bloodline

If you are Isreal, the chosen one- accept & operate in all My principles
If JESUS be the Son of GOD, your Savior- walk steadily and truly in CHRIST' footsteps

If I AM KING of Kings, LORD of Lords- show its through the fruits of your actions not only in your lips

If you plan to live with Me in eternity- Praise Me now!

If you love Me- Do My will, not yours relinquish your religious pre-occupation

Embrace the opportunity
Find out the man you were intended to be
Stop short of changing yourself
Learn fully to LOVE somebody else
There is no shame
In learning a new game
LOVE! LOVE! LOVE! Emotional LOVE

IN SPIRIT and IN TRUTH

Before we know where we are going
We must understand who we are
Who we really are deep down inside
Where are our ancestors buried?

What tribes & roots do we spring from
Where our ancestors slept at night
I'm referring to 3rd-10th generations
You know! Those 7th grand-parents

Who did they pray to and worship
We must honor our ancestral traditions
We must understand where we came from
In order to understand where we're going

What gods are we serving today?
Is it power, prestige and/or lust?
Lust of eyes, of flesh, pride of life
Original garden of Eden sins

We're made by Almighty GOD
Called JEHOVAH or ABBA
Nevertheless let every man
Call on His own GOD

GOD hears & answers prayers
We worship the one true GOD
One GOD in spirit and in truth
We call on Him since our youth

There will come a day
On mountain tops
Cities, churches, temples
Worship GOD in spirit & truth

Bow your heads, please
Tell GOD your needs
He supersedes all our
Feeble attempts to fix it

GOD will do it for you
We are like His children
We are His sheep
GOD! ABBA! ABBA!

GOD is a spirit!   Praise GOD!   All praise, honor   Amen

IT'S REAL

Oh! How well do I remember
How I doubted day by day
For I did not know for certain
That my sins were washed away

But the spirit tried to tell me
The truth I would not receive
Endeavor to be happy
And make myself believe

Praise GOD!
        All my doubts
                Are settled
                        I know it's real!

JESUS came today!
While you were out!
JESUS came today!
HE passed this way!

JESUS came today!
HE agreed!
We looked the other way
I heard someone say!

JESUS came today!
We were ever so near!
Near to the soon coming KING!
HE came to stay!

Well! How did HE look?
Who knew? Light too bright!
Where did HE stand?
Over there by the brook?

No! One foot on the mountain top!
The other in the bottom of the abyss!
With outstretched pierced hands
Come over here! Take a look!
Amen!   Amen!

JESUS! SOON COMING KING!

Our soon & coming KING!
Master of everything!
Hosanna! Host of angels sing
Heavenly bells ring!

Clouds of glory descend
Angels chants
JESUS has come again!
Dead in CHRIST ascend!

Hallelujah! Amen!
Hallelujah! JESUS came again!
Hallelujah! Our personal friend!
Hallelujah! On earth you descend!

Death! Where is your victory!
Grave! Where is your sting!
Hallelujah! All praises bring!
Blessings throughout world fling!

JESUS! My personal Savior!
Holy Ghost! Comforter to the end!
Risen Savior! We recommend!
So be it ! Amen!

Back to heaven!
We will all go!
Loved ones reunion
We'll meet you know!

Take JESUS the painkiller
Take JESUS your tranquillizer
Take JESUS your Savior, friend
Take JESUS your equalizer

Take JESUS Holy Ghost empowered
With blessings you'll be showered
Our precious Savior
Go tell your neighbor

JESUS! LORD! KING of Kings!
JESUS! heavenly angels sing!
JESUS! heavenly Savior!
"Love thy neighbor" (Matt 19:19)

Into kingdom of heaven on earth
Let JESUS in your heart! Rebirth!
Yes! JESUS! Come in! LORD!
Read daily GOD's anointed Word!

Take Jesus everywhere you go
 Alpha and Omega
Greatest man on earth, you know
Your personal Savior

JESUS is the pain killer, you know
JESUS heals, cures, sets free
JESUS, LORD, personal Savior
"Love thy neighbor!" (Matt 19:19)

Hallelujah! Praise GOD! Hallelujah!
"gospel your feet are shod" (Esp 6:15)
Yes! JESUS! KING of Kings! Yes!
JESUS! Be born again!

Yes! JESUS loves me and you, too
What can mankind without HIM do?
Yes! JESUS! Supreme sacrifice!
JESUS! We don't have to die twice!

Hallelujah! Praise GOD
"With gospel of peace our feet are shod" (Esp.6:15)
Hallelujah! Praise GOD!
Read daily GOD's infallible Word!

AMEN! AMEN!

JUST SAY NO

Just say "No!"
That the way to go!
Just say "No!"
No way! No way to show!

No need to show!
Up looking for me!
On the corner
To deal dope anymore!

I cannot continue to kill
Myself & friends
I love life!
I love my neighbor as myself

I love GOD!
Who first loved me!
Forgive me!   LORD!
Save me! JESUS!

In the name of JESUS!
I pray!
Save me today!
Come into stay!

Amen!   Amen!   Hallelujah!

Pain Killer | 47

KILLING FIELDS

What did he or she do?
Pull the plug! *"PtP"
I thought just had heart trouble
Cause of death- broken heart!

Oh! Yeah! It is cheaper!
Than to keep him or her here
We can't afford to maintain life
So we'll chose death! "PtP"!

It certainly is because
Anyone can get tired of you
And say off with his head
I mean "PtP" instead!

What was the condition again
In spite of the long tedious list
It's summed up in the three words!
Pull the plug! Pull the plug!

What new term is that?
Oh! It's so simple! Family members
Talk with the Dr. & decided
To pull the plug! No hope! No point!

Some choice!
Some choice words!
Pull the plug!
Sounds worse than cancer!

How gruesome, cold and unkind
It's plain & simple murder
While they sit all in a neat row
At funeral that they didn't have to go

What plug! The plug of hope in life!
The plug of self-worth & dignity!
The plug of desire to live!
The love plug!

Shut down all systems! Close all doors of escapes hatches! Notify the nurses & aides!	Isn't this fun! Guess what? Your trouble has just begun You should have been tried for murder!
Let's play games! Pull the plug!	Condemned guilty! Serving time!

Murder is murder! That's all to it!	*"To me belongs vengeance…* *(Deu. 32:35)*
There's nothing polite or intellectual About it! Murder is murder!	*"There is no god with me:"* *"I kill and I make alive…"* *(Deu. 32:39)*
Especially your Mother or Father!	Hallelujah! Amen! Amen!

LET OTHERS

Praise GOD from whom all blessings flow
LORD! We thank You for storms, temptations
GOD! We thank You for Your Son, JESUS CHRIST!
Praise GOD for sending salvation to us below

JESUS CHRIST! Our personal Savior!	Praise GOD!
JESUS CHRIST said love your neighbor!	Praise the LORD!
JESUS CHRIST laid down His life for all men!	Praise GOD!
JESUS CHRIST died and rose again!	Praise the LORD!
JESUS CHRIST! Paid the price!	Praise GOD!
JESUS CHRIST! "You'll deny Me trice!"	Praise the LORD!
JESUS CHRIST! GOD in the flesh!	Praise GOD!
JESUS CHRIST was sent to bless!	Praise the LORD!
CHRIST JESUS! The risen KING!	Praise GOD!
CHRIST JESUS! Hosanna! Wes sing!	Praise the LORD!
CHRIST JESUS! Soon coming KING!	Praise GOD!
CHRIST JESUS! He's coming again!	Praise the LORD!

Let Your Word come alive in me!
Let others, JESUS, you in me see!
Let others be drawn to the Word!
Let others say, "Praise GOD!"

Let other's see JESUS in me!   Praise GOD!
Let other's be drawn to Thee!   Praise the LORD
Let other's fall at my hand!   Praise GOD!
Let other's hear! Be born again!   Praise the LORD!

Let others no longer live in sin!
Let others, repent, be forgiven, be born again!
Let others know CHRIST suffered & died for us!
Let others know CHRIST is a must!

Let others believe on the LORD CHRIST!
Let others know JESUS saves sinners!
Let others know JESUS loves you!
Let others know JESUS will see you through!

Believe on LORD JESUS CHRIST!
Let others believe He died! Paid the price!
Let others believe GOD' Son sacrifice!
Let others shout, "GOD is for me!"

Let others say, "Praise GOD!"
Let someone say, "Amen!"
Let others testify, "Holy Ghost, I received!"
Let someone testify, "I believe!"

Let it be me! LORD!
Let it be me! LORD!
Let it be me! LORD!
Oh! GOD! Let it be me! Amen!

LET THE HEALING FLOW

Thank GOD for yet another year
Yes! 364 days! Hallelujah!
In spite of being lied to & deceived
Disappointment! Heartache! Death!

Thank GOD for yet another!
Yes! 364 days! Hallelujah!
HE's been with me thro' it all
HE encouraged me to stand tall!

Yes! All is vanity! These human ways!
Doing things to each other
I'll never understand fully
While saying they love each other

Is it love to lie, steal & destroy?
Feelings of trust & confidence
Is it fair to bear false witnesses
Against your loved one?

Yes! Thank GOD for another 364 days!
Thanks everyone who passed my way
Thanks to all who tried

Thanks to all who stood by my side

Thanks to loved ones & friends
Thanks to those who passed on
Thanks to those who are yet to be born
So why cry? Why mourn?

Look up! Laugh! Live!
Open your heart! Just forgive!
Look around at the sea of faces
Open your mind! Expand! Go to new places!

Seek new faces! Seek new places!
Set new goals! Look to new horizons!
Set out anew with fresh dry eyes!
Set out one step at a time!

Come on! Just this march thro' life!　Life each moments as if it's the last!
Come! Little ones! Stop bickering & strife!　Yes! It's the last time! It's Past!
Come! Let's get started on another 365!　Yes! One blink! Oh! What a gas!
Live each moment!　Yes! Life is a challenge! It's fun!

So put down pills, dope liquor　After all we're only human!
Put down those knives & guns　Full of so many mistakes!
Let the past go!　Wrong thoughts & statements!
Let Forgiveness flow!　Just waiting to happen!

Each day us a brand new start!　So what! Forgive me, please?
Each day is a new dawn!　So to cause you Dis-Ease!
Just another breath we take!　Displeasure! Offensiveness!
Ooops! There goes another mistake!　It's all vanity! Just a silly mess!

Thanks! Forget it!　Enjoy life!　Praise GOD!
Everything is all right!　It's a blast!　Hallelujah!
Breathe! Relax! Chill out!　Count down! Contact!　Praise GOD!
There's no need to go up tight　Blast off!　Hallelujah! Amen!

LIVING and FORGIVING

This is with warm greetings that
You extend each day to each and
Everyone, who passes your way
Greetings like a sun shiny day!

Here are prayer
Heart felt prayers
Winging their way!
Each day! Hallelujah!

Dear LORD! Thank You for
Each tests, trial, tribulation
Dear Lord! Thank You for
The year of jubilation

The 50th year when
Debts are forgiven!
When al transgression
Are forgiven!

So we can keep on living and forgiving
Living and forgiving
FATHER! Forgive them because
They know not what they are doing!   Amen! Amen!

LORD BE MERCIFUL

LORD be merciful unto me! 3x
Lift me up out of the pits
Of despair & grief
Save me! Oh! LORD!

Hold me up! Oh! LORD!
With Your outstretch arm
Shield me from all harm!
Send relief! Cover me!

Protect me from attacks!
Show me the way back!
Hear me as I cry inside!
Send Holy Ghost as my guide!

Save me from every constant fear!
Deliver me from rejections here!
JESUS! Keep me near the cross!
Help me, LORD, not to be lost!

Oh! GOD is able! Fix it! 2x
Oh! GOD can! Fix it! 2x
Heal it! 3x GOD!
Fix it! 3x LORD!

Deliver us from evil, LORD!
JESUS! 7x LORD! 7x   2x
My GOD! LORD! My Sheppard!
My shield! Thy will! 3x

This is his last time
Walking with ungodly
This is His final walk
LORD today! 7x

FATHER
My GOD!
Sky! 8x
Pray! 8x

See! Pray!
Select! Say!
Regain! Remain!
Recoup! Regroup!

Pain Killer | 55

Release! Release!   Rectify!   Rejoice!
Rediscover! Recover!   Refuse!   Restore!
Receive! Reseal!   Refute!   Reiterate!
Reply! Rely!   Recession!   Rebate!

Recognize! Reorganize!   Reserve! Refill!
Rescind! Resent!   Repossess! Resell!
Review! Reasser!   Revamp! Revive!
Reuse! Refuel!   Thank You! 44x Amen!

MAN WHO

Oh! GOD! Thank You for David!
A man after GODs heart!
GOD! Thank You for David!
Seeker after GOD's heart!

A man who sought justice & truth!
A man who loved GOD from his youth!
A man who relied on Your word
A man who looked for answers from above!

A man who sought Your face everyday!

A man who loved GOD!

A man who believed & feared!
A man who knelt to pray!

A man who looked to heaven each day!
A man who understood what it means to pray!
A man who obeyed GOD!
A man who received GOD's nod!

A man who felt GOD's grace!
A man who sought GOD's face!
A man who saw miracle working power!
A man who tasted deliverance hour!

GOD deliver us from evil!
GOD deliver us from the devil!
GOD deliver us from friend & foe alike!
GOD deliver us thro' blood of CHRIST JESUS!

Hallelujah! Praise GOD!
Deliver us from all evil, dear LORD!
Cover us, JESUS, with Your precious blood!
Hallelujah! Praise GOD! Hallelujah!

        Amen!

Thank GOD for His living Word!
David sought kingdom of GOD!
And it righteousness
All else shall be added unto you! 2x

        Amen!

MISSION FOR CHRIST'S SAKE

Call me out!   LORD!
Cast me out!   LORD!
Cover me!   LORD!
Deliver me!   LORD!

Forgive me! LORD!
Heal me! LORD!
Help me! LORD!
Keep me! LORD!

Protect me! LORD!
Reveal to me! LORD!
Separate me ! LORD!
Show me! LORD!

Kill the old me, LORD!
Project me into the things you want me to be!
Reveal to me Your precious secrets!
Teach me where you want me to be, LORD!
Tell me again that You love me, LORD!

Bless You, LORD!   Glory to GOD!   Hallelujah!   Thank You!   Amen!

My GOD! My GOD!
Why hast Thou forsaken me?
My GOD! My GOD!
Why have You left me?

My GOD! My GOD!
How I trust You!
My GOD! My GOD!
You've created me!

My GOD! My GOD!
You've cleansed me!
My GOD! My GOD!
You've favored me!

My GOD! My GOD!
You've healed me!
My GOD! My GOD!
You've helped me!

My GOD! My GOD!
What is happening to me?
My GOD! My GOD!
Oh! How I love You!

My GOD! My GOD!
You've adored me!
My GOD! My GOD!
You've blessed me!

My GOD! My GOD!
You've girded me!
My GOD! My GOD!
You've guided me!

My GOD! My GOD!
You've increased me!
My GOD! My GOD!
You've inspired me!

My GOD! My GOD!
You've loved me!
My GOD! My GOD!
You've multiplied me!

My GOD! My GOD!
You've projected me!
My GOD! My GOD!
You've protected me!

My GOD! My GOD!
You've sanctified me!
My GOD! My GOD
You've saved over me!

My GOD! My GOD
You've strengthened me!
My GOD! My GOD!
You've watched over me!

My GOD! My GOD!
Set my feet on high places!
My GOD! My GOD!
Hide me from scourge of my enemies!!

My GOD! My GOD!
Be gracious unto me!
My GOD! My GOD!
Give me peace!

My GOD! My GOD!
Through all these years!
You've never forsaken me!
You've never left me!

Thank You JESUS! My LORD!
For You are truly my friend!
You're my soon coming KING!
Oh! How I love You!

Thank You JESUS! My LORD!
I love You! I adore You!
I worship You!
I surrender to You totally today!

Forgive me of all my sins!
Wash me in Your precious blood!
Cleanse me whiter than snow!
Save me! Receive me into Your kingdom!

I will worship You!
In spirit! In truth!
My soon coming KING!
Hallelujah! Amen! Amen

NEW WAVE OF MY HEALING

A new wave of my healing
"...healing in his wings..." (Mal. 4:2)
Get ready for a new wave of healing
Miracles unlike never been seen before!

"...Eye has not seen, nor ear heard...
The thing which the GOD " (1 Cor. 2:9)
"...wisdom, and righteousness (1 Cor. 1:30)
Do greater works !

Do the works that I give you
With all your might!
"Fear not : for I Am with you...
Will uphold you with ...righteousness "(Is. 41:10)

Hallelujah! Praise GOD! Hallelujah!
Praise GOD! Praise You JESUS!
Thank You! Hallelujah!
So be it according to Your Will!   Amen!

No other help
Unto You, oh GOD, do I lift my hands
No other help I know! Oh! GOD!
My LORD! Show us which way to go!

In the morning! In the evening! All day long!
Place in our hearts, oh GOD, a new song!
Glory to GOD! Glory! My LORD!
Glory to GOD! JESUS! The living Word!

Hallelujah! Praise GOD!
Hallelujah! Praise the LORD!
Hallelujah! Praise GOD!
JJESUS! JESUS! JESUS! My LORD!

Unto You we lifted our hands!
Send Your peace upon our land!
Let Your perfect Will be done
Thank GOD for our daily new birth

Daily we die to CHRIST
GOD's supreme sacrifice
Glory! Glory! Glory to GOD!
Hallelujah! Praise the LORD! 2x

LORD! Look upon us!					Holy Ghost! Give us nod!
LORD! Have mercy on us!				Praise GOD! Amen!

"Seek first the kingdom of GOD and his righteousness and all else will be added unto you"

No good thing will Your heavenly Father withhold
What does this exactly mean?
What is the kingdom of GOD?
What does this conditions of righteousness mean?

What is the bread un leaven ?
Who are the wheat & tariff yield?
What is the field?
Who is the over thrower?

What means these parables?
What do these parables mean?
Where is the sense of it?
Who are the counterfeits?

If you wanted to buy a precious stone
Would you not sell all
To get it
Everything

SURRENDERED LIFE

The surrendered life
With your Savior, JESUS CHRIST
Surrender completely to Your will
Become the bride of JESUS CHRIST!

Surrendered life! You don't die twice!
Don't have to die twice
Surrendered life! JESUS CHRIST!
Supreme sacrifice!

Surrendered life!
JESUS CHRIST! Paid the price!
Surrender your life!
Live CHRIST-centered life!

Surrender! 3x
Render!   3x
Unto the LORD!
For all His benefits

What shall I render
Unto the LORD?
For all His benefits
Surrender! 3x

Sanctified! Set aside!
Holy Ghost spirit filled!
Accept GOD's perfect will
Surrendered life!

Surrender your heart
With all your might
Make a brand new start
Hold onto JESUS CHRIST tight

Cling to His pierced bleeding side
Let Holy Ghost teach & be your guide
Read daily GOD's infallible Word!
Live a CHRIST-like life!

Glory to GOD! Hallelujah!
Praise the LORD!
Hallelujah! Praise GOD!
Hallelujah! Praise the LORD!

Glory to GOD! Hallelujah!
JESUS CHRIST is LORD!
Glory to GOD! Hallelujah!
GOD's anointed Holy Word!

Glory to GOD! Hallelujah!
JESUS CHRIST! GOD's anointed Word!
Hallelujah! Praise GOD!
"Gospel of peace your feet are shod"
(Eph. 6:15)

Glory to GOD! Hallelujah!
Hallelujah! Praise GOD!
"Seek first the kingdom of GOD"
Praise your KING! CHRIST the LORD!

Hallelujah! LORD!
Hallelujah! Praise GOD!
Hallelujah! Glory to GOD!
Thank You LORD! Amen!

OBEDIENCE TO GOD

Obedience to You! GOD!
Work assignment from you
Evenly yoked in marriage
Obedient! Loving children!

Anointed career! Music! Singing!
Financial abundance!
Multi-business
Missions for sake of JESUS CHRIST!

Anoint me! LORD!	Forgive me! LORD!
Appoint me! LORD!	Heal me! LORD!
Call me! LORD!	Help me! LORD!
Console me! LORD!	Keep me! LORD!

Protect me! LORD!	Sanctify me! LORD!
Receive me! LORD!	Save me! LORD!
Renew me! LORD!	Seal me! LORD!
Revive me! LORD!	Send me! LORD!

Show me! LORD!   Bless You! LORD!
Teach me! LORD!   Glory to GOD!
Tell me! LORD!   Praise You, JESUS!
Visit me! LORD!   Thank You, LORD!

Cast more of me out of Your prefect way!
Project me into things You want me to be!
Reveal to me! Your precious secrets!
Tell me again that You love me!   Hallelujah!   Amen!

ON CALVARY

Praises to you in the name of the LORD
Praises to you from above
Praises to your family!
Praises to your deepest please!

Praise to your secret heart's desire
Praises to your soul's fire!
Praises to your every dream!
Praises to things closer than they see!

On Calvary JESUS died
On Calvary they pierced His side
On Calvary were sins forgiven
On Calvary roads were paved to heaven

On Calvary with His stripes we are healed
On Calvary eternity was revealed
On Calvary JESUS was crucified
On Calvary JESUS suffered and died

On Calvary Mary wept
On Calvary other crept
On Calvary many ran away
On Calvary others prayed_

On Calvary one thief saw GOD
On Calvary JESUS shed water & blood
On Calvary JESUS life was relinquish
On Calvary, JESUS cried, *"It is finished!"* (John 19:30)

On Calvary JESUS breathed His last and died
On Calvary gushed water and blood
On Calvary John JESUS; Mother took
On Calvary earth and heaven shook

Calvary!   3x
Prophesy!   3x
Redemption! 3x
Salvation!   3x

LORD JESUS! Look down on us from above!
LORD JESUS! Look down on us from above!
LORD JESUS! Look down on us from above!
LORD JESUS! Look down on us from above!   Amen!   Amen!

ONLY YOU

Cause Your face
To shine upon us
LORD our Savior!
Prince of Peace!

We love You!
Almighty One!
Begotten Son!
Coming KING!

Thro' the storms
Thro' tests of time
Thro' the come-ons
Thro' the crimes

Thro' accusations
Thro' indecisions
Thro' insecurities
Thro' inquisitors

Thro' insincerity
Thro' lost money
Thro' money spent
Thro' trouble sent

Thro' alibis
Thro' all the lies
Thro' mind disorders
Thro' troubled waters

Thro' dangers unseen
Thro' in betweens
Thro' envious friends
Thro' secret sins

Thro' bad times
Thro' chastisements
Thro' loud cries
Thro' mistreatment

Thro' I did my best
Thro' emotional upsets
Thro' hopelessness
Thro' mental perplex

Thro' foolish decisions
Thro' guilt floods
Thro' inoperative words
Thro' personal prisons

Answer us! LORD!
Deliver us! LORD!
Embrace us! LORD!
Examine us! LORD!

Heal us! LORD!
Hear us! LORD!
Help us! LORD!
Hide us! LORD!

Protect us! LORD!
Reach us! LORD!
Save us! LORD!
Seal us! LORD!

Thro' crafty schemes
Thro' crazy dreams
Thro' predicaments
Thro' imprisonment

Thro' what's going on
Thro' same old songs
Thro' sounds like
Thro' lies being told

Find us! LORD!
Free us! LORD
Greet us! LORD!
Guide us! LORD!

Judge us! LORD!
Keep us! LORD!
Look on us! LORD!
Meet us! LORD!

Seek us! LORD!
Teach us! LORD!
Touch us! LORD!
Try us! LORD!

"Surely, I come quickly! Amen! Even so, come, LORD JESUS!" (Rev.22:20)

LORD JESUS CHRIST and soon coming KING! Praise GOD! Amen! Amen!

OUTCRY FROM SILENT LIPS

An outcry from silent lips
An outcry from helpless
An outpouring of distraught distress
An unbelief & grief thro' yet another test

Put your hand in GOD's, my dear son!
And leave it there
Don't retract or even flinch
Put on new man thro' CHRIST JESUS!

Old things are past away
"...Behold I make all things are new..." (Rev. 21:5)
Be renewed daily with mind of CHRIST
That is the resurrected LORD JESUS CHRIST

Do not look back to former things
Do not think about old things twice
Move forward with CHRIST!
All will be well!

Well done! My beloved son! Well done! My beloved son! Amen!

PLACE CALLED THERE

A place called there! No
Right/wrong answers
Only right "Now!"
The "Now! Now!"

How do you find it anyhow?
Where do you look?
Who do you ask?
Can you find it in a book?

Or I the question you ask?
Maybe? It's the answer?
This place's called, "There!"
Perhaps! Maybe! Probably!

It's beyond the moon
Just past the stars
Into unknown galaxies
Or is it in me?

Is it where the dew?
Embraces the sea mist?
The sky kisses earth
Where is it?

Yes! It's in each others hearts
As we seek the face of GOD!
Yes! It's His security!
It's our divine destiny!

It's our dedicated obedience!
It's we embrace abstinence
It's in our selfishness
When we have sinful wishes

It's our chastisement
When His will's fulfillment!
It's in trials & tribulations
We bow down in nations

We bow before the KING!	It's when every eye shall see!
As heavenly bells ring	As we on bended knee!
When His kingdom comes	Honor! Praise! Glory! Oh! KING!
And His will be done!	His kingdom now seen!

We ask frequently	We gaze intently	We fast reverently!
We pray reverently	We openly sign	We fight fiercely!
We sang about it	We cry softly	We prat fervently!
We seek diligently	We stare silently	We wait patiently!

We mourn	We're kingdom citizens!
We persist steadily!	We're liberated in eternity!
We whisper softly	Hush! Or we forget!
We shout loudly!	Whom the Son sets free!

Bondages! Curses! Mind sets!	Is free indeed!
We're Free! Free! Free!	Hallelujah! So be it! In JESUS' name! Amen!

Praise GOD for persistence
Praise GOD for insistence
Praise GOD for stead fastness
Praise GOD for standing stress!

Praise GOD for determination!
Praise GOD for decisive action!
Praise God for sincerity!
Praise GOD for tears shed secretly!

Praise the LORD for frequent stops!
Praise the LORD for false starts!
Praise the LORD for commitments
Praise the LORD for sentiments!

Praise GOD for your concerns!
Praise GOD for silent yearns!
Praise GOD for visions & dreams!
Praise GOD for ways & means!

Praise God for cheerfulness!
Praise GOD for cleverness!
Praise GOD for business sense!
Praise God for help from whence!

Your help comes from whence!
The LORD! Yes! You LORD! My LORD!
Blessings showered from above!
Yes! You show my beloved love!

Yes you! Yes you! Yes you!
What and why did you do?
You gave her heart's desire!
You now feel your soul set free!

You'll be on fire for CHRIST!
You'll glow the rest of your life!
For I touched you with a special touch!
Oh! You'll be blessed so much!

You'll be blessed, blessed, blessed!
You'll confess, confess, confess!
You'll old friends, associates & fears!
You'll add time to your years!

As you wonder what to do!
An angel is already on the way!
With an answer to your dismay!
GOD is going to open windows on you!

Yes! Windows of blessings!
Showered from above!

Blessings showing
GOD is love!

GOD! Thank You for brothers in CHRIST!
Help them live a CHRIST like trusting life!

Trusting GOD sufficiency for all needs
GOD know & sees every deed!

"Fret not yourself of evil doers neither be afraid…" (Psalms 37:1)
The keeper of Israel does not slumber or sleep!" (Psalms 121:4)

Don't fret over evil doers!
Don't be dismayed!
Don't try old feelings to renew!
Let them cut short their days!

Trust me more & more!
Seek Me! Open the door!
The door to your heart!
The door to your soul!

Give me your all
I'll give you your needs!
Answer business dilemmas!
Answer secret endeavors!

I will protect you!
From callousness!
From cold heartedness!
From all criticism!

I will protect you!
From callousness!
From cold heartedness!
From all criticism!

JESUS will fix it!
GOD is able!
JESUS will fix it!
GOD can! AMEN!

"Bless you my dear sons!

"Fear not for I AM with you… for I AM thy GOD…" (Isaiah 41:10}

Pray as never before!
Pray GOD will open closed doors!
Pray secretly & sincerely
Pray for loved one dearly!

Pray to heaven above!
Pray to touch GOD's love!
Pray never ceasing!
Pray fervently!

Pray to JESUS!
Pray to CHRIST!
Pray to Holy sacrifice!
Pray open heartedly!

Pray daily!
Pray devoutly!
Pray frequently!
Pray openly!

Pray! 7x	Oh! LORD! 7x	Have mercy ! 7x
Pray! 7x	Oh! LORD! 7x	Have mercy! 7x
Pray! 7x	Oh! LORD! 7x	Have mercy! 7x
Pray! 7x	Oh! LORD! 7x	Have mercy! 2x

Dear JESUS!
Come into my heart!
Take away all my sins
Wash me in Your blood
Give me the Holy Ghost
Write my name in the lamb's book of life
In JESUS' name!   Amen!

Say, "Hallelujah!"
(With uplifted hands)

REPENTANCE! RECONCILIATION!

We need revival thr'out this nation!
Let's try repentance & reconciliation
JESUS prayed on the cross?
FATHER! You are the boss!

What did JESUS pray in Gethsemane?
"…but as Thou wilt…" (Matt.26:39)
What did JESUS pray on the cross?
"…I commit My spirit…" (Luke 23:46)

JESUS as You stared out from Calvary
"FATHER! Forgive them." (Luke23:34)
Remit their sins! Forgive them!
Prince of peace! Supreme sacrifice!

Lamb of GOD! Ultimate divine sacrifice!
"FATHER!" JESUS said as He looked
Across humanity. *"…into Thy hands
I commit My spirit!"* (Luke 23:26)

As You gazed into eternity
"It is finished!" (John 19:30)
Now all mankind can join
GOD's heavenly community

Brothers & Sisters! Why are you killing
Forgetting your sisters & brothers?
Yes! We are our brother's keeper!
Love on earth can't get no deeper

Love on earth like no other
JESUS! My brother!
Love on earth like no other!
JESUS! My brother!

While hanging on the cross, He moaned
"FATHR! Forgive them.!" (Luke 23:34)
They pierced His side! He groaned!
"Why hast Thou forsaken Me."

There is no need to fear! With the remission of sins! Through the precious Shed blood of JESUS!	The Son of GOD! Our ultimate sacrifice! GOD forgives our sins We must be born again
Believe on the LORD JESUS CHRIST! And you will be saved Believe on the LORD JESUS CHRIST! And you will be saved	REPENT! FATHER forgive me! RECOUNCIL-FATHER give me another chance! RESSURECTED – Power of JESUS CHRIST! FATHER empower me to a living witness!
They overcome by blood of the Lamb And the word of our testimony LORD JESUS! Come into my heart today! I believe You died for me!	Let Your light so shine on me! LORD JESUS! Set me free! From bondages of sin & death! Here on earth for all eternity
Come dear JESUS! Set me free! Come Holy Spirit! Dwell in me! Come into my heart LORD JESUS! Come Holy Ghost! Empower me!	Praise the living GOD! Oh! Glory! Glory to GOD! Hallelujah! Praise the living GOD! Oh! Glory! Glory to GOD! Hallelujah!
Come LORD JESUS into my heart! Come LORD JESUS! Give me a new start! Come LORD JESUS into my heart! Come LORD JESUS! Give me a new start!	LORD JESUS! I repent of my sins! FATHER! Remit my sins! CHRIST JESUS reconciles! JESUS' resurrection power! Amen!

SAVED BUT NOT SERIOUS

How long have you been saved?
Seven years? No! Seventy!
What have you done for the LORD!
I'm saved, sanctified, filled with Holy Ghost!

What have you done for JESUS?
I'm satisfied living Holy!
Is He satisfied with you?
Are you sanctified, too?

What can I do?
Get on your knees! Cry Master!
Show me? Tell me what to do!
GOD has a plan for you, too!

Get Saints! You have a job to do!
Saints! You have commandments!
Saints! You have an appointment!
Saints! Go into the world! Preach!

Glory to GOD! 2x Hallelujah!
Let GOD! Work through you
Glory to GOD! Praise the LORD!
More Holy Ghost power to you!

Get more serious with GOD!
Get more serious with you Savior!
Get more serious with being saved!
Get in the harvest! Be a laborer!

"…your feet shod with preparation of the gospel of peace." (Eph. 6: 15)
Glory to GOD! Praise the LORD!
More Holy Ghost power to you!

"Be not weary of well doing." (2 The.3:13)
"Fear not…confounded." (Is. 43:2)
"Fret not yourself…of evil doers (Ps. 37:1)
JESUS' precious blood paid ultimate price!

Hallelujah! Praise GOD! 2x   Praise GOD! Praise the LORD!
Hallelujah! Praise the LORD! 2x   Hallelujah! Read GOD's Word!
With gospel of preparation peace   Hallelujah! Get into harvest fields!
Your feet are shod! Amen! Amen!   Hallelujah!   Work for the LORD!

Amen!

SOAKING IN JESUS' LOVE

I love you with an everlasting love!
Love eternal! Love immeasurable!
Love emended! Incredible! Indescribably!
Undefinable! Incredible! Injunctive!

So awesome! So insightful! So profuse!
So passionate! So promising!
Fulfilled with compressed
Moved to compassion!

Wait, again, I say, "Wait on Me!"
Hear my voice! Obey my Word!
Do My Will! In season! Out of season!
Come close! For "I AM coming soon!"

Your love is calling Me back!
Your prayers, faith, trust in Me
Longs for the spirit of truth! Comforter!
To rest, rule in your hearts richly

Oh! GOD! My strength! My Holy Redeemer!
I hear You, LORD! I feel You!
I will obey and trust! Hallelujah! My LORD!
Not my will, but Thy Will!   70x 7   Amen!

SPIRITUAL HOMELESSNESS

The stench of homelessness
Pain of abandonment
Shameful predicament
Guilt! Hopelessness!

Broken hearts mending
Death pending
Sins lingering
Souls wandering

Elect us!
Guide us!
Lead us!
Protect us!

What about spiritual homelessness?
What about hope deferred?
What about soul's restlessness?
What about no living Word?

JESUS! Come into my heart!
I choose to make a new start!
Come into my heart, LORD JESUS!
Forgive me! Save me! Deliver me!

To become Your chosen vessels
In Your arms we rest!
Under the shadow of Your wings we nest!
In secret place we seek Your face!

Thank You, LORD!
Thank GOD!
Praise You, LORD!
Thank GOD! Amen!

STAND ON THE WORD

"Put on the helmet of salvation, breast plate of righteousness....(Eph. 6:11)

Stand on the Word
Spirit of truth! Let your lions be gird!
"Put on the helmet of salvation
Breast plate of righteousness

"Feet shod
Put on the two edge sword
Shield of faith to quench every fiery
Dark of the enemy..." 2x

With JESUS on your side you can be set free!
Hallelujah! Free base! 3x Based on freedom in JESUS!
Hallelujah! Free base! 3x
Based on freedom in GOD's kingdom!

Free base! Uh..hum Hallelujah! Glory to GOD!   Get mad at the devil
Free at last! Get GOD' wink & nod!   Give your heart to CHRIST!
Free at last! Hallelujah!   Get mad at Satan
Whom gods would destroy 1st they make mad_   Turn away from evil!
                                                                                        Hallelujah!

Get mad at the devil!   Get mad at evil!
Refuse to be destroyed!   Turn away! Turn aside!
Get mad at Satan! Praise GOD!   Shun all works of the devil! Hallelujah!
Start daily reading GOD anointed word!   Let the Holy Ghost be your guide!

Turn away! Turn around! Turn your life Snatched back form pits of hell!
To CHRIST JESUS! Your soon coming KING! Give your heart to JESUS! Glory to GOD!
Be free from Satan's wiles! Make a clean, new fresh start! Glory!
Hallelujah! The angel sing! Give your heart to JESUS!

Free at last!
Great GOD Almighty!
Free at last!
Thank you! JESUS! Amen! Amen!

SUDDENLY JESUS

Suddenly JESUS came into my life!
Certainly JESUS made me His new wife!
Suddenly JESUS took all my sins away!
Certainly JESUS can set you free today!

Suddenly JESUS brought the light, the truth!
Certainly JESUS showed me the way!
Suddenly JESUS saves children, adults, youth
Certainly JESUS can set you free today!

Look out for dark shadows in your life
Watch that you don't die twice
"But seek first the kingdom of GOD…" (Matt. 6:33)
Find the complete #7

"Judge not…" (Matt. 7:1)
"Love ye one another…" (Jn. 15:12)
"Seek ye first kingdom of GOD…" (Matt. 6:33)
Find the complete #7

Plan to give your heart to JESUS *"Love GOD with all your heart ..."* *(Matt.22:37)*
Please GOD not man!
Reach out! Give JESUS your heart!

Praise GOD! Hallelujah!   2x
Be saved today!   2x
CHRIST JESUS is the way!   2x
Praise GOD! Amen! Amen!   2x

THANK GOD

Thank You for lighting up my life
Thank You for making personal sacrifice
Thank You for obeying spirit of GOD
Thank you for "Hello" with wink & nod

Thank You! Brightening my day!
Thank You! Showing me a new way!
Thank You for inviting me in
Thank You for your smiles & grins

Thank you for your positive approach
Thank you for not taking any, "No's"
Thank you for your persistence
Thank you past pains setting me free

Thank GOD for you, my dear friend
Thank GOD for new beginning, no end
Thank GOD for friendship last eternity
Thank GOD for relationship heavenly

Thank GOD! No misunderstandings can separate
Thank GOD! You're my GOD sent soul mate
Thank GOD for my GOD given husband   Glory!
Thank GOD for a GOD fearing husband   Hallelujah!

Thank GOD for a salvation friend
Thank GOD for he is born again
Thank GOD for a second chance
Thank GOD upward mobility advance

Thank the LORD for you!
Thank the LORD for a friend so true!
Thank the LORD for friend tested & tried!
Thank the LORD on whom many relied!

"May the LORD watch between you and me while we are absent one from another! " (Gen.31:49)

"Fret no yourself because of evil doers, neither be afraid…" (Ps 37:1)

"Be not weary of well doing…" (2 Thess. 3:13)

Take care of your dear self! JESUS has set us free! Be free! Stay free! In JESUS' name! Amen! Amen!

THY WILL

Praise the LORD!
Praises to the most High GOD!

Praise You! LORD!
Love You! GOD!

My *"FATHER which art in heaven*
Hallowed be Thy name
Thy kingdom come
Thy will be done…" (Matt.6:9)

Thy will! oh LORD!
Not mine!   2x
Thy will! Oh LORD!
Not mine! Thine not mine!

Hallelujah! Praise GOD!
Hallelujah! Praise GOD!
Oh! GOD! Glory to
Your precious name!

Praise the LORD!
Glory to GOD!
Hallelujah!
Amen! Amen!

TOUCH NOT MY ANOINTED

"...Touch not my anointed, and do my prophets no harm." (Psalm 105:15)

Yes! Touch not! Do no harm!
Yes! Do not gossip or back bite!
Bear false witness! Slander!
Against my anointed vessels

Thus says the LORD!
Yes! Do my prophets no harm!
Vengeance it mine!
Touch not! Speak not against!

Prophets on a mission from GOD
Do not need a person's nod
Nod of approval
Frown of disapproval

Touch not mine anointed!
Those whom I have appointed!
Those whom I called and qualified!
Do not back bite, watch and tell lies!

Touch not mine anointed!
Do my prophets no harm!
Thus says the LORD!
Those feet are gospel shod!

Touch not mine anointed!
Touch not those whom I've appointed!
Touch not mine anointed!
Those whom I've appointed!

Hallelujah!   Amen!

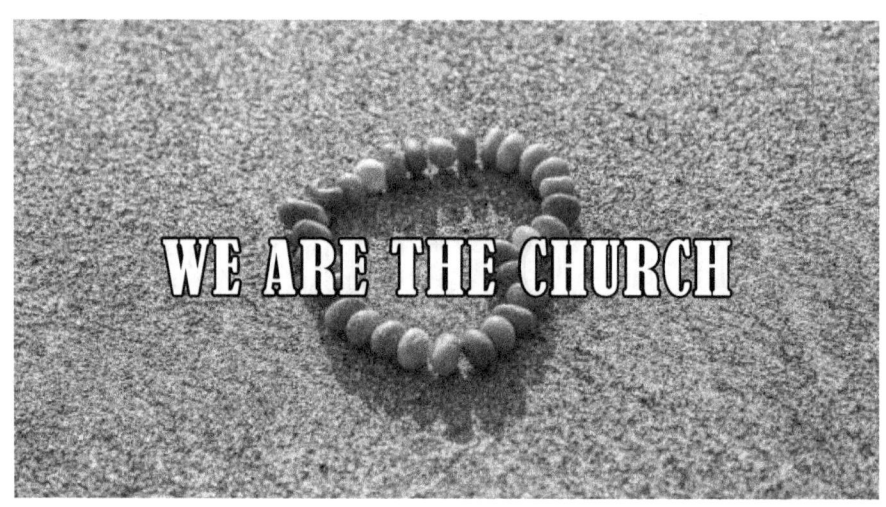

WE ARE THE CHURCH

We are the church!
JESUS is coming soon!

We are body of CHRIST JESUS!

Who rose from the dead to free us!

To free us from oppression & sin
To free us from ourselves! We're born again!

We're the body of CHRIST! Holy Ghost filled!

We will not die twice!

We're the church without walls!
We stretch across the world!

Gospel of peace our feet are shod!
As the banner of CHRIST unfurls

As our spirits touch from shores to shore!
As Holy Ghost fires travel coast to coast!

As winds of GOD blow heart to heart!
With JESUS, we have brand new start!

As GOD' power speaking in tongues!

Ring out & mighty outpouring begun
Upon our sons & daughters, who prophesy!
We see signs & wonders in the sky!

We know our help comes from on high!
We believe GOD' infallible Word!
We trust GOD! Our LORD! Our Savior!
We look to the author & finisher of our faith!

With JESUS we know our place!

We are in this world! Not of it!

We are sanctified! Set aside!

For our soon coming KING!

Hallelujah! 3x Glory to GOD! Heavenly host sing!

Hallelujah! 3x Glory to GOD! Heavenly host sing!

JESUS!   KING JESUS is coming back again!

JESUS!   Almighty great GOD JEHOVAH JIRA!

Hallelujah 3x	Praise GOD!	Hallelujah! 3x	Praise the LORD!
Hallelujah! 3x	Glory to GOD!	Hallelujah! 3x	My Savior! Crowned KING!
Hallelujah! 3x	Praise the LORD!	Hallelujah! 3x	Anointed One!
Hallelujah! 3x	KING of KINGS!	Hallelujah! 3x	GOD' only begotten Son!

Hallelujah! Glory to GOD!   Amen!

WHAT IS MAN?

"That we should be saved from our enemies…" **(Luke 1:71)**
…have not h into heart of man… things … GOD
has prepared for them…! *(1 Cor. 2:9)*

That Thou art mindful of him?
A little lower than angels
What is man? Is he a priest?
A priest in his household?

Hallelujah! Glory to GOD!
"Your feet shod…
gospel of peace " (Eph.6:15)
Praise! LORD! My GOD!

Shelter from a storm
As storms of life raging
JESUS stands to say
"Peace be still!" 2x

A little lower than an angel
But with power & dominion
Over all earthly creatures
Even women! Yes! Women!

His Eden! His garden of prayer
His overcoming spirit
His conquering conquest
His mighty high tower

More than a conquer!
More than an emperor!
More love to Thee
More love to Thee!

Man is made in the image of GOD
What is the true essence of GOD
What is man that You
Oh! GOD! Are you mindful of him?

Woman was made from man!
From man's rib! For man'
Pleasure was woman created
For GOD' pleasure, we're created

To worship & adore GOD! To praise & adore GOD! To be fruitful & multiply! To rule & have dominion!	Great are Your tender mercies! Great is Your love! You gave Your only begotten Son that Whosoever believes will be saved
Thank GOD! Man's stabilizing Force in my life high tower Rock! Fortress! Strong Protection! Shield! Strength!	Thank GOD for man Thou art mindful of him Turn heart of man To His heavenly Father
Thank You! FATHER GOD! In the midst of any storm! We cry out to You! You hear & will answer!	Save us from all our iniquities Forgive us our transgressions Spare us from pestilences Deliver us from fowlers snares
You, GOD, are the light of my life You, GOD! My strength & shield! You, GOD! My mighty high tower! You, GOD, are my hiding place!	We can hide under the Shadow of Your wings We can gather next to You As a hen gathers her chicks!

"When you have done this unto the least of them,
you have done this unto Me!" (Matt 25:30)
"Remember the LORD in the days of your youth and when
you are old you shall not depart…" (Ecc. 12:1)

We love You, LORD! 2x Through our spouse Through our children Through our loved ones	LORD! I will not depart from you! I will not depart from You! You, JESUS, are the vine We are the branches
And our love will grow And bear much fruit Fruits of righteousness! Spirit, body & mind!	And Your love will surely grow! Forever! Forever! As you know *"I am the vine! You are the branches!" (John 15:5)* *"I will abide in you and you abide in Me!" (John 15:4)*

"My love shall abide in you!" You know you will grow! Hallelujah! 2x
"My love shall abide in you!" You know you will grow! Hallelujah! 2x

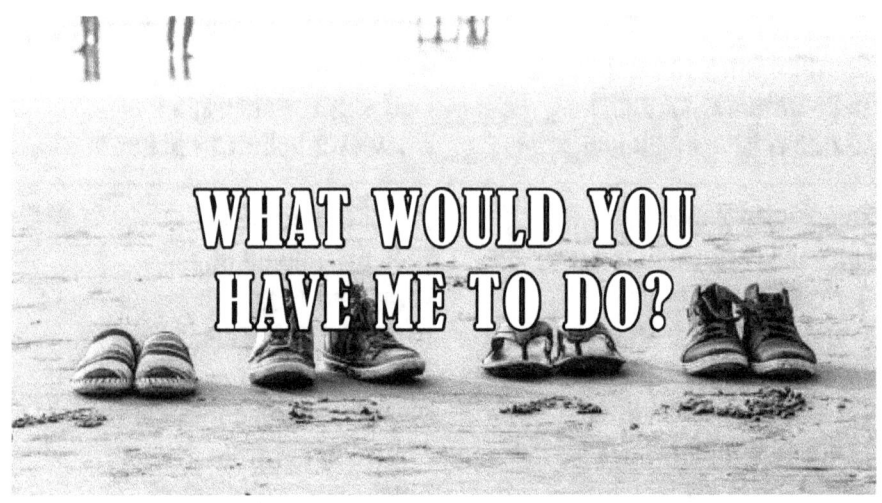

WHAT WOULD YOU HAVE ME TO DO?

What would you have me to do?
Create a safe, sound environment
For my son to become a man
That You destined him to be

GOD gave me an anointing
HE opened my heart so I could see
Feel the words HE was saying
The truth of His feelings

GOD open my eyes
So I might see
HE is truly doing
With His actions

GOD open my ears
So I can listen
Carefully! Hear clearly!
Things HE is verbalizing!

Most of all I became opened
And very vulnerable
Arrested from myself
Released into His custody!

This is by no means easy
Believing! Practicing!
I can do anything
Better! Who needs you?

I can't stand you!
But my body needs you!
I don't believe a word
I hear you talking! You liar!

You came along as I was
Being swept down sewage
In torment of insanity
You, JESUS, rescued me!

Pulled me ashore	Emotional fire of warmth
Put me in your truck	I will help you!
Drove me to your house	I'll take you where
Lite a fire in the hearth	You need to go
This is against my wishes!	I sat near warm fires of
Thoughts! Desires!	Compassion, caring, concern
Cause I have nowhere to go!	I stared at my pain & sorrow
I was numb & in shock!	Told deep remorseful stories
I shared my dreams!	Cried out! GOD help me!
Sometimes truth hurts!	Be open! Receive GOD's love!
I uttered my sorrows!	GOD! I'm so hurt & angry!
Flash backs engulf my mind!	Help me! Believe GOD' love!

Thank You, JESUS!   Thank You, LORD!   Thank You, JESUS!   Thank GOD! Amen!

WHERE DO WE GO FROM HERE?

Where do we go from here?
When no one your problem can see?
Who do we turn to?
When friends & enemies leave you?

What do you do
When Satan's demons you pursue?
What can you say?
Help me LORD! I pray!

What do you do when bills are due?
When no money can be found?
When lenders are begging the borrowers?
When nobody with any money is around

What you do quietly is
Stretch your hands to GOD Almighty!
What can you say?
Have mercy on me today

Where should you go?
When ill winds and trouble blow
When alcohol, dope or sex can't get you high
When turmoil lurks in an over cast sky

What do you do quickly
When problems make you sickly
What can I say? Hallelujah!
LORD! Give me strength always!   Praise GOD!

WORSHIP HIM!

Blessing the in the name of the LORD!
Blessings! Blessings! Showered from above!
Blessings! Showing GOD's love!
Blessings! Proclaim CHRIST's shed blood!

Oh! JESUS paid it all!
Oh! JESUS made the call!
Oh! JESUS said, "Come to Me!"
Oh! JESUS! Set us free!

Thank You!   7x

Call Him!   7x
Claim Him!   7x
Praise Him!   7x
Serve Him!   7x
Worship Him!   7x

With all you might!   Oh! GOD!
Get a new start!   Oh! LORD!
Praise the LORD!   Oh! JESUS!
Worship Him in higher heights!   Amen! 7x

"Lo! I am with you unto the ends of the earth…" (Matt 28:20)

You can't take the place of GOD!
I will not give up GOD for you!
I love GOD with all my heart!
So I must obey GOD in all things!

"LO! I am with you unto the ends of the earth" (Matt 28:20)
Wedges driven between us of unbelief & disobedience
Can only be removed by me by confessions
Forgive me! All the hatred & resentment

Forgive me! Trying to use GOD!
GOD to get me ahead in life!
Take charge of me & my life!
Let Your abundant life explode inside of me!

Come in, LORD JESUS!
Come into my heart now!
Occupy until JESUS comes!
Thank You, LORD! Hallelujah!

Glory to GOD! Amen! Amen! Amen!

www.ingramcontent.com/pod-product-compliance
Lightning Source LLC
Chambersburg PA
CBHW071527080526
44588CB00011B/1587